Fun with WALDO

Based on the characters created by
MARTIN HANDFORD

Little, Brown and Company
Boston Toronto London

Well, here we are Waldo Watchers at Emeralda's birthday bash. Everyone is enjoying the party except Odlaw! Can you find out how old she is today? Here's your clue:

Count the dogs in the picture,
Take away all the darts,
Add this to the number of mud men,
And the number of hearts.

Good luck! And by the way, Emeralda is holding a white handkerchief.

DID YOU KNOW?

The pulp of one tree is needed to make 40 copies of a single newspaper.

Natural forests once covered nearly two thirds of the world's land surface, but clearing land for agriculture has reduced this to barely one third.

Trees are among the largest and oldest living things in the world. The tallest tree in the world is growing in Redwood Creek Valley, California. It is 367 feet tall and about 46 feet round.

A Rocky Mountain Bristlecone tree is said to be 5,000 years old!

Did you know that each state has its own flower and bird? Find out which is your State's bird and flower and draw them in a crowd scene of your own neighborhood.

THINGS TO DO

1)
3)
2)
4)
5)

Can you match up the names of the trees which these leaves are from:

A) **SYCAMORE,**
B) **BEECH,**
C) **ASH,**
D) **OAK,**
E) **BIRCH.**

Ahoy, O sharp-eyed shipmates. Just look at this captivating crew! While I hop on board and practice my pirating, there's a little problem I'd like you to solve. I'm on the lookout for a priceless emerald ring. Can you help me find it? Here's the clue:

**The purloining pirate
Has a very large nose,
No hair on his head,
And no shoes for his toes.**

Good luck, oh, and after you've guessed who the ring really belongs to, how many things can you find beginning with the letter "P"?

DID YOU KNOW?

Blackbeard the pirate's real name was Edward Teach. He used to put burning rope in his long beard to terrify his victims.

A pirate's favourite drink is Grog, a mixture of rum and water.

To avoid a nasty disease called scurvy, English sailors used to eat limes. The name "Limey" is still used today to describe an Englishman.

There were women pirates, too, of course. Two of the most terrifying were Anne Bonny and Mary Read, who both plundered the Seven Seas!

Pirates rarely made their prisoners walk the plank. It was far better to put them to work as crewmen.

THINGS TO DO

Try untwisting these tongue twisters by saying each one as fast as you can:

Tattooed traitors taking tea
Thieving treasures
Tee Hee Hee!

Sailing on the seven seas, sixty salty seadogs saw some snooty sea serpents.

Pirate Peg Leg pinched a piece of priceless precious plunder.

Making merry maps for mighty marooned mariners.

Persia used to be the name of the country we now call Iran.

Aladdin, Sinbad, and Ali Baba are all characters from a set of stories called the "Thousand and One" or "Arabian Nights" which were written in the 15th century.

The greatest King of Persia was Darius. He built a series of roads 1,680 miles long. The Kingdom could be crossed by the King's horsemen in one week! It would have been quicker by magic carpet, of course!

Darius' bodyguards were called "The Ten Thousand Immortals" and were expert warriors.

PUZZLE:

Subtract the number of Ali Baba's thieves from the number of Arabian Nights, and then add the voyages of Sinbad. What do you get?

Way to go Wacky Watchers! Just look at the fantastic fun these friendly fellows are having! There can only be one explanation for all of this magical mayhem:

This is the work of a genie, Of that there can be no doubt! But you'll have to look carefully for him, As he lives in a home with a spout!

Take your time and find the genie's house and then look for his pet mouse! Whitebeard says you should be able to do this in less than a minute, so good luck and happy hunting!

Can you match these shadows to the people in the picture? Look carefully because two of the shadows are reversed!

Because of the wide variety of food and the unchanging climate in the South American rain forest, the birds there are more abundant and brightly coloured than anywhere else on Earth.

The tapir is a relation of the horse and the rhinocerous. It sleeps during the day and feeds at night!

The Pygmy Marmoset is the smallest monkey in the world. It grows to only 3-4 inches in length!

The loudest monkey in the world is the Howler monkey. Its cry can be heard for many miles.

The Vampire bat lives in the rain forest. It is called this because it drinks the blood of animals while they are asleep! Yuk!

Jumping Jungle Jimminies! All these animals! How many can you recognize O Wise Waldo Watchers? But the animals might be in danger:

The Aztecs have raided the Jungle,
Looking for something quite rare.
It's blue and white, and it flutters,
Find it, and warn it "Beware!"

Count the number of monkeys in the picture and repeat out loud "Mishchievous, Madcap, Monkeys making mayhem" quickly until you solve the riddle.

THINGS TO DO

Try and replace the pieces of these pillars correctly ? Be careful because one of them doesn't fit at all!

Heavens! Head Honcho Hunter really knows how to throw a party! But I can't stay and play as Wenda has asked me to find two things which she left behind in all the fun:

**To keep my head warm,
My hat you must get,
But I've also lost something,
To stop getting wet!**

Well, any ideas? Off you go, and by the way there are 2 hats which could be Wenda's so perhaps we'd better find both, just in case!

THINGS TO DO

All the letters of the alphabet are numbered for you. To find out the name of the person I'm thinking about all you have to do is match the number of things I'll ask you to find to the letters and then juggle them a bit:

the number of playing cards with blue backs
the number of marshmallows
the number of hunters with moustaches
the number of light bulbs
the number of hunters playing leap frog.

DID YOU KNOW?

The story of St. George and the Dragon dates from the 3rd century and is believed to be based on the exploits of a man who lived in Palestine at that time.

Hercules killed a dragon with many heads called a Hydra.

A tail eating Dragon is used as a symbol of life in Eastern countries.

A short musket or rifle of the 16th and 17th centuries was called a Dragon. Hence the man who used it was called a Dragoon.

The Kimodo Dragon is not a dragon at all, but a huge lizard over 6 feet long!

The Chinese celebrate the year of the Dragon. The next year of the Dragon will be from the year 2000 to 2001.

A 1 B 2 C 3 D 4 E 5 F 6 G 7
H 8 I 9 J 10 K 11 L 12 M 13 N 14
O 15 P 16 Q 17 R 18 S 19 T 20 U 21
V 22 W 23 X 24 Y 25 Z 26

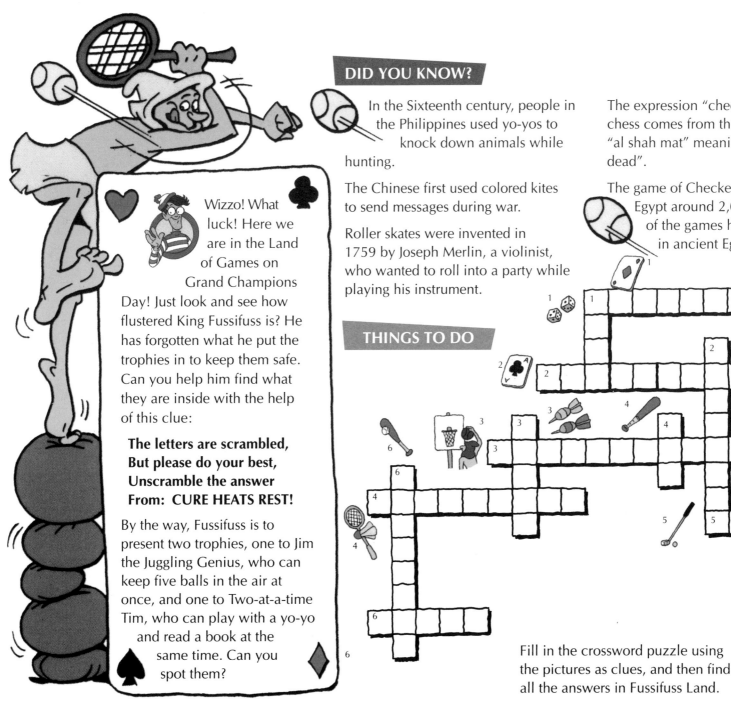

Wizzo! What luck! Here we are in the Land of Games on Grand Champions Day! Just look and see how flustered King Fussifuss is? He has forgotten what he put the trophies in to keep them safe. Can you help him find what they are inside with the help of this clue:

The letters are scrambled,
But please do your best,
Unscramble the answer
From: CURE HEATS REST!

By the way, Fussifuss is to present two trophies, one to Jim the Juggling Genius, who can keep five balls in the air at once, and one to Two-at-a-time Tim, who can play with a yo-yo and read a book at the same time. Can you spot them?

DID YOU KNOW?

In the Sixteenth century, people in the Philippines used yo-yos to knock down animals while hunting.

The Chinese first used colored kites to send messages during war.

Roller skates were invented in 1759 by Joseph Merlin, a violinist, who wanted to roll into a party while playing his instrument.

The expression "checkmate" used in chess comes from the Arabic phrase "al shah mat" meaning "the King is dead".

The game of Checkers was invented in Egypt around 2,000 BC. Examples of the games have been found in ancient Egyptian tombs.

THINGS TO DO

Fill in the crossword puzzle using the pictures as clues, and then find all the answers in Fussifuss Land.

Woof and I really look forward to Saturday night at the Rocksy.

Everyone is rolling up to see "Rockbo," the latest rockbuster epic starring Sylvester Stone. Someone is causing mischief in the audience though - can you spot him? He's holding a mouse. He has hidden something from Cary Granite the movie theater manager. Can you discover what and where it is? Here's a clue:

When you are hungry,
I have a hunch,
You wouldn't be happy,
To be missing your lunch!

Well, be as quick as you can – the action will start as soon as the sun goes down!

DID YOU KNOW?

The Paleolithic, or Old Stone Age began about 500,000 years ago!

The dinosaurs had disappeared about 130 million years before the first man arrived!

The Paleolithic period ended when the Ice Age (about 8,000 years ago) changed the climate of the world.

Stone Age man probably first appeared in Africa and Asia.
Ancestors of the American Indians crossed from Asia to Alaska, which were once connected by land.

In states such as Arizona, Colorado, and Massachussetts we have found many arrow-heads used to kill Mammoths. They were still there after 7,000 years. Wow! Perhaps someone should speak to their street cleaner!

THINGS TO DO

How many words of three letters or more can you make out of the letters in the word Paleolithic? There are at least 100 so don't give up!

When I crave an extraterrestrial treat, the long journey to Space City is certainly worth the spaceship lag! On such a great visit it's a shame to have someone who could ruin our wonderful day. Can you find who it might be:

She's wearing strange glasses,
And shoes that are blue.
She's looking for someone,
I hope it's not you!

There's only one creature in the Universe who can eat more hamburgers than Woof. It's Hungry Horace Space Hog. He is wearing a red ribbon around his neck. To find out how many burgers Horace can eat, add the number of shakes to the number of robots.

DID YOU KNOW?

The largest meteorite to have reached Earth landed in Namibia, southern Africa. It weighs over 66 tons! But before it entered the Earth's atmosphere, it probably weighed 88 tons.

Haley's comet is seen every 76 years or so. It is about the size of Manhattan and was shown in the Bayeux Tapestry flying over the Battle of Hastings in 1066.

It takes only a few days for a spacecraft to travel to the Moon. But to reach Jupiter (360 million miles away), it would take more than a year.

If the distance between the Earth and the Sun were one inch, the nearest star would be about four and a half miles away.

THINGS TO DO

Draw a space creature and a space helmet like this on a piece of cardstock. Fold it in half and thread two thick rubber bands through the holes shown. Wind up the rubber bands and then let them unwind at eye level and see the creature inside the helmet!

① FOLD

② HOLE PUNCH

③ THREAD BANDS

④ LOOP

⑤ TWIST

⑥ SPIN!

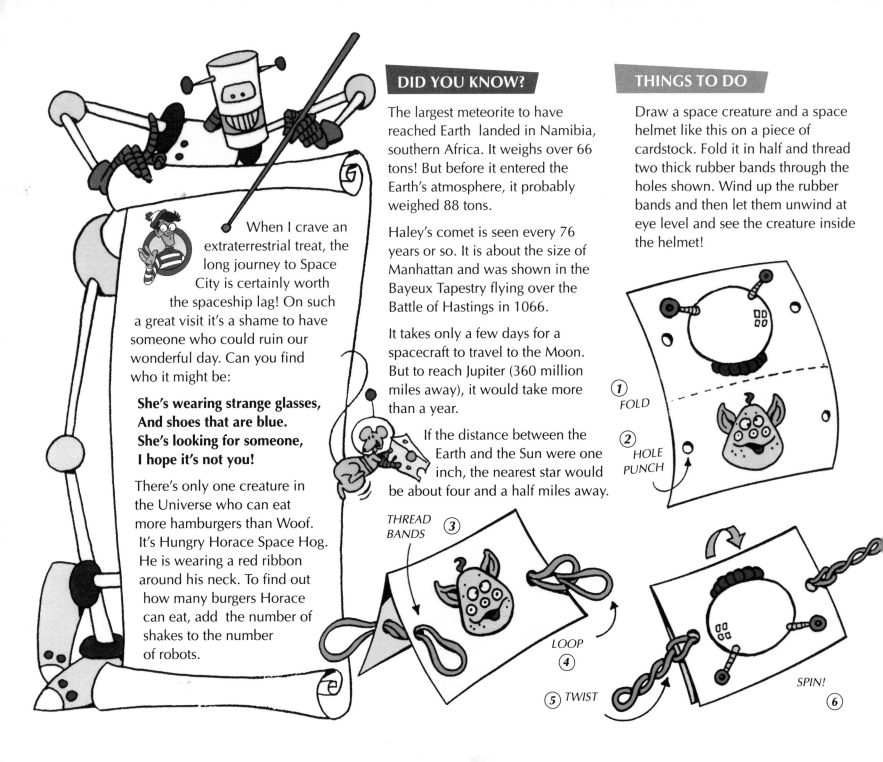

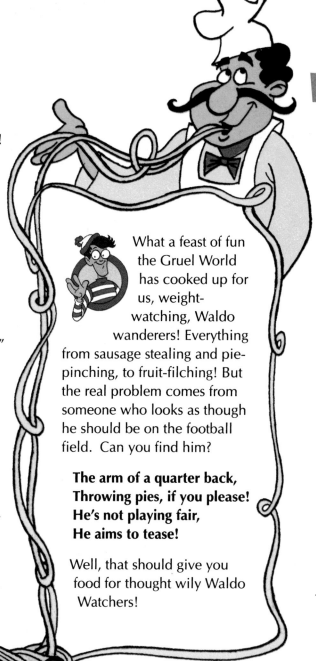

DID YOU KNOW?

Gruel is a thin soup made by boiling oatmeal in water, or sometimes milk! Mmmmm! Tasty!

Popcorn was invented at least 5,000 years ago by American Indians. In 1510 Columbus and his men brought popcorn necklaces from natives in the West Indies back to Europe.

The first pies were made in Ancient Greece. They were called "artocreas" or hash meat pie and they did not have a top crust!

You might think that pasta was invented in Italy, but no! It really comes from China. It is supposed to have been brought back to Italy by the Polo brothers, Maffeo, Niccolo, and his son Marco, in about 1300 AD.

The word "cereal" which is used to describe any edible grain such as wheat, oats, or corn, comes from the name of the Roman goddess of agriculture, Ceres.

What a feast of fun the Gruel World has cooked up for us, weight-watching, Waldo wanderers! Everything from sausage stealing and pie-pinching, to fruit-filching! But the real problem comes from someone who looks as though he should be on the football field. Can you find him?

The arm of a quarter back,
Throwing pies, if you please!
He's not playing fair,
He aims to tease!

Well, that should give you food for thought wily Waldo Watchers!

THINGS TO DO

Something has gone wrong with these items from Chef Baker Cook's kitchen. Can you take them apart and put them together again properly? What should they be?

_ _ _ _ _ _ _ _

_ _ _ _ _ _

_ _ _ _ _ _ _ _

_ _ _ & _ _ _ _ _ _ _

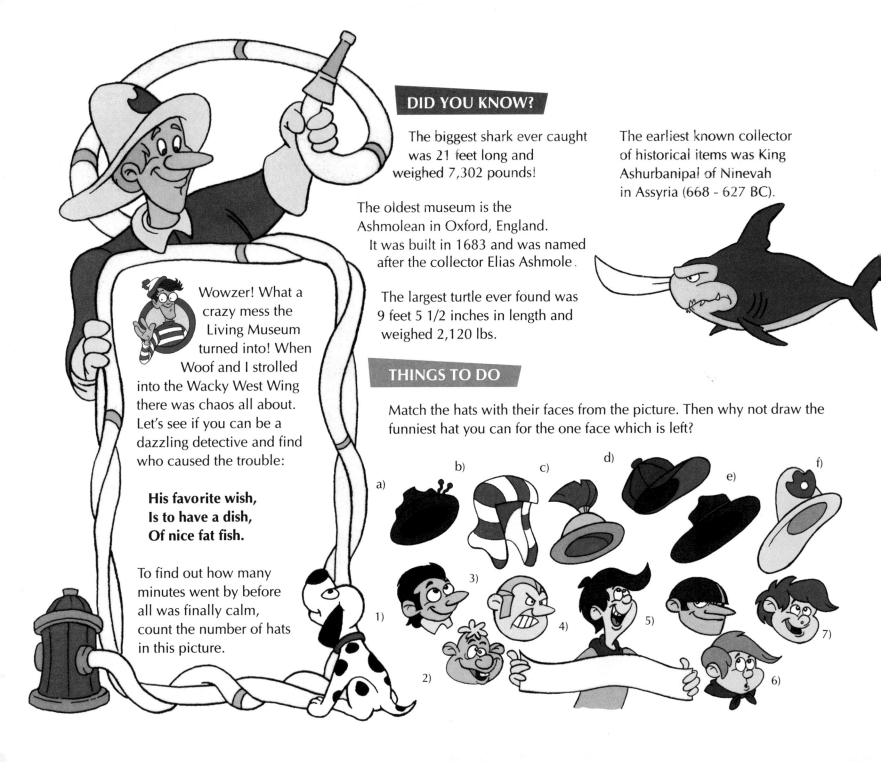

DID YOU KNOW?

The biggest shark ever caught was 21 feet long and weighed 7,302 pounds!

The oldest museum is the Ashmolean in Oxford, England. It was built in 1683 and was named after the collector Elias Ashmole.

The largest turtle ever found was 9 feet 5 1/2 inches in length and weighed 2,120 lbs.

The earliest known collector of historical items was King Ashurbanipal of Ninevah in Assyria (668 - 627 BC).

Wowzer! What a crazy mess the Living Museum turned into! When Woof and I strolled into the Wacky West Wing there was chaos all about. Let's see if you can be a dazzling detective and find who caused the trouble:

**His favorite wish,
Is to have a dish,
Of nice fat fish.**

To find out how many minutes went by before all was finally calm, count the number of hats in this picture.

THINGS TO DO

Match the hats with their faces from the picture. Then why not draw the funniest hat you can for the one face which is left?

a) b) c) d) e) f)

1) 2) 3) 4) 5) 6) 7)

CHECK LISTS

PIRATES

- [ ] A Heart tattoo
- [ ] A Teddy bear
- [ ] A Pair of glasses
- [ ] A Pair of scissors
- [ ] A Cup of coins
- [ ] A Feather
- [ ] A Ship's wheel
- [ ] A Vain pirate
- [ ] 2 Sword fish
- [ ] 1 Eye-patch
- [ ] 2 Books
- [ ] 2 Golden Crowns
- [ ] A car tire

AZTECS

- [ ] 3 Sloths
- [ ] 2 White birds
- [ ] 2 Anteaters
- [ ] A Man juggling fruit
- [ ] 4 Parrots
- [ ] 2 Men eating bananas
- [ ] A Butterfly net
- [ ] A Falling pot
- [ ] 2 Jaguars
- [ ] A Man pulling tongues
- [ ] 5 Men in stripy skirts
- [ ] A Book

GREEN FOREST WOMEN

- [ ] A Table lamp
- [ ] 2 Feathers
- [ ] A Television set
- [ ] 3 Candles
- [ ] A Golf club and ball
- [ ] 3 Unicorns
- [ ] A Chicken drumstick
- [ ] A "Diamond"
- [ ] A Teapot
- [ ] A Bird on a dog's nose
- [ ] A Mud slinger
- [ ] A Mud catcher
- [ ] A Slippery cake
- [ ] An Ace of spades
- [ ] A woman with scissors
- [ ] A Sleeping bird

FLYING CARPETS

- [ ] A Snake
- [ ] A Carpet surfer
- [ ] 2 Hitchhikers
- [ ] A Cowboy
- [ ] A Needle and thread
- [ ] A Box of oranges
- [ ] A Fruit thief
- [ ] A Bag thief
- [ ] A Turban with scissors
- [ ] 2 A Turban feather
- [ ] A Clothesline
- [ ] 2 Shopping baskets
- [ ] 2 Pairs of yellow shoes
- [ ] A Bunch of grapes

UNDERGROUND HUNTERS

- [ ] A Striped rug
- [ ] A Pillow
- [ ] 2 Ice creams
- [ ] 3 Ladders
- [ ] 6 Dartboards
- [ ] 1 Bow
- [ ] 1 Kite
- [ ] 1 Television set
- [ ] 1 Painting
- [ ] 1 Light bulb
- [ ] 10 Spears
- [ ] 1 Cactus
- [ ] 1 Blonde huntress